Cents From the Heart

Cents From the Heart

Journal

Tinuke Aweda

WestBow
PRESS
A DIVISION OF THOMAS NELSON

WestBow Press books may be ordered through booksellers or by contacting:

WestBow Press
A Division of Thomas Nelson
1663 Liberty Drive
Bloomington, IN 47403
www.westbowpress.com
1-(866) 928-1240

Because of the dynamic nature of the Internet, any web addresses or links contained in this book may have changed since publication and may no longer be valid. The views expressed in this work are solely those of the author and do not necessarily reflect the views of the publisher, and the publisher hereby disclaims any responsibility for them.

Any people depicted in stock imagery provided by Thinkstock are models, and such images are being used for illustrative purposes only.

Certain stock imagery © Thinkstock.

ISBN: 978-1-4497-4548-6 (sc)

Library of Congress Control Number: 2012905983

Printed in the United States of America

WestBow Press rev. date: 4/25/2012

Seyi & Bimbo: Love leaves a memory no one can steal

Mum & Dad: You have dared mighty things …and won glorious triumphs

Wumi & Bisi: The contrary winds drive our roots deeper

GONE.....

She sat in her chair on her porch
Watching as the sun set and the moon took its place
Rocking..Rocking…Rocking her chair
Her eyes were opened but I could tell she saw nothing
Her mind had wandered again
I watched and waited wandering what story she had
today
Finally, after a thin smile played across her lips
My grandmother broke the silence and said
"Where did the world go"?
That was all she said...
I was left alone to answer her question
I could not but wander what world she meant
To me the world has always been around us
So what did she mean
I would never forget the pain in her eyes as she walked
away
Still deep in thought
One thing was sure
She was not talking about this world I see
So what world did she mean?
And where did it go?

_____

_____

_____

_____

_____

_____

_____

_____

_____

_____

_____

_____

_____

_____

_____

_____

_____

_____

_____

_____

_____

_____

_____

_____

_____

_____

Tinuke Aweda

_____

_____

_____

_____

_____

_____

_____

_____

_____

_____

_____

_____

_____

_____

_____

_____

_____

_____

_____

_____

_____

_____

_____

_____

_____

_____

_____

_____

_____

_____

_____

_____

_____

_____

_____

_____

_____

_____

_____

_____

_____

_____

_____

_____

_____

_____

I WAS BORN

What is brighter than the sun?
What is steeper than a mountain top?
The world with all its glory and splendor don't compare
To the eternal beauty that radiates
Radiates with every smile
Every embrace
Every wink of the eye
That is how I know you stand alone in your class
And you have chosen me to be the object of your affection
I walk with my head high everyday
Knowing that with you by my side and your approval in
everything I do, there is no stopping me
And so I reach farther, I search deeper trying to know
why you have chosen me
Chosen me to lavish this affection on
The only answer I get each time I ask, is that the reason
for my selection is that I was born
Not because I have a sweet voice
Not because I can sing or write
Just because I was born
That is why the father has chosen to shower me with so
much love
What more can I ask for
Knowing that the master and owner of the universe has
my best interest at heart

_____

_____

_____

_____

_____

_____

_____

_____

_____

_____

_____

_____

_____

_____

_____

_____

_____

_____

_____

_____

_____

_____

_____

_____

_____

_____

_____

_____

_____

_____

_____

_____

_____

_____

_____

_____

_____

_____

_____

_____

_____

_____

_____

_____

_____

_____

_____

Tinuke Aweda

_____

_____

_____

_____

_____

_____

_____

_____

_____

_____

_____

_____

_____

_____

_____

_____

_____

_____

_____

_____

_____

_____

_____

_____

_____

_____

_____

_____

_____

_____

_____

_____

_____

_____

_____

_____

_____

_____

_____

_____

_____

_____

_____

_____

IF I COULD

If I could, I would pick a star to give your eyes a glow
If I could, I would take a picture of you smiling
That is all I need to bring hope to a dying child
If I could I would write your name on the sands of time
That way, the world will always remember you came
If I could, I would sit by you all night to watch you sleep
Watching as the first ray of sunlight touches your face;
PRICELESS
But I can't. So I have to be content with watching you
from afar
Wishing and praying that you will notice my presence,
my stare
Praying that one day, as the elevator gets to the 4th floor
And you step out, your face will turn to mine
Praying, just praying that my prayers will be answered
If I could, I would give anything for that moment
That one moment when the whole world would stand still
when you say to me
Where have you been all my life

_____

_____

_____

_____

_____

_____

_____

_____

_____

_____

_____

_____

_____

_____

_____

_____

_____

_____

_____

_____

_____

_____

_____

Tinuke Aweda

Tinuke Aweda

_____

_____

_____

_____

_____

_____

_____

_____

_____

_____

_____

_____

_____

_____

_____

_____

_____

_____

_____

_____

_____

_____

_____

_____

KNOWING AND NOT KNOWING

There's a thin line between knowing and not knowing
Seeing and not seeing
Hearing and not hearing
Feeling and not feeling
So thin is the line that once you cross it there is no going
back
You always want to know, see, hear and feel
It's like a whirlpool
It drags you in deeper and deeper
Even when you know you should not go any further
But, like gravity you can't help yourself
It pins you down like a spider's web on its prey
Only a miracle
A miracle as it is called is what brings you out
And once you come out of that web
You have to live with the scars for the rest of your life
Knowing, that there's a thin line between knowing and
not knowing
Seeing and not seeing
Hearing and not hearing
Feeling and not feeling
And once you cross that line
There's no going back

_____

_____

_____

_____

_____

_____

_____

_____

_____

_____

_____

_____

_____

_____

_____

_____

_____

_____

_____

Tinuke Aweda

_____

_____

_____

_____

_____

_____

_____

_____

_____

_____

_____

_____

_____

_____

_____

_____

_____

_____

_____

_____

_____

_____

_____

_____

_____

_____

_____

_____

_____

_____

_____

_____

_____

_____

_____

_____

_____

_____

_____

_____

_____

MEMORIES

Sway to the left
Sway to the right
Lift your hands, close your eyes
Feel the melody, dance to the beat
The drums rolling bringing out music
Like magic to the eyes and medicine to the heart
The night is young just as you are
So dance, laugh, clap, jump
Feel the rhythm, feel the beat
Dance till your limbs hurt
Dance till all left is joy and laughter
And when the music stops and the dance is over
Keep the memories of the night forever
Keep the memories of the music, of the dance, of the
laughter
So on the day there is no music to liven the heart
You can reach within to memories of time past
Memories of laughter and dance
Memories of rhythm so sweet it touches the heavens
In it find the strength to laugh again
In it find the courage to dance again
Till another night comes and fresh memories are stored to
be kept forever
To be remembered at all times

Tinuke Aweda

_____

_____

_____

_____

_____

_____

_____

_____

_____

_____

_____

_____

_____

_____

_____

_____

_____

_____

_____

_____

_____

_____

_____

_____

_____

_____

_____

_____

_____

_____

_____

_____

_____

_____

_____

_____

_____

_____

_____

_____

_____

_____

_____

REINS

I have always thought that life will always create the op-
portunity for you to achieve your dreams
I got that from many people around me
But soon I realized that you are your life
Living in your space and observing your nature
Your life is what you make of it
No one will hand over the reins to lead your life to you
The reins to lead your life is the air you breathe
Once you have it
You can achieve anything you want
Anytime you want
So keep breathing

Tinuke Aweda

_____

_____

_____

_____

_____

_____

_____

_____

_____

_____

_____

_____

_____

_____

_____

_____

_____

_____

_____

_____

_____

_____

Tinuke Aweda

_____

_____

_____

_____

_____

_____

_____

_____

_____

_____

_____

_____

_____

_____

_____

_____

_____

_____

_____

_____

_____

_____

SAGES

People say sages are very wise people that walk the face
of the earth
I think so too
But what turns a man into a sage
Is it his ability to see what others don't see?
Is it his boldness to say what others can't say?
Is it his courage to go where others can't go?
Is it his tenacity to endure what others can't endure?
WHAT
After thinking through, I've come to this conclusion
A sage is a man that turns opportunities into achievements
That sees farther than the eyes can see
That speaks words carefully woven together by mastery
That dares to go beyond the finish line
That is a sage
Where can he be found
He is in every heart
He is in every brain
He is in every soul
But only the brave dares to bring him out
Are you brave?

_____

_____

_____

_____

_____

_____

_____

_____

_____

_____

_____

_____

_____

_____

_____

_____

_____

_____

_____

_____

_____

_____

Tinuke Aweda

Tinuke Aweda

_____

_____

_____

_____

_____

_____

_____

_____

_____

_____

_____

_____

_____

_____

_____

_____

_____

_____

_____

_____

THE CHILD

I stood
And I looked around
All I could find was a land
So rich
Filled with children
That had no hope no means for survival
Everyone looked at them and walked past
Never caring about their future
But deep in the heart of the lord
I can hear him say
Give them hope
Show them love
There's so much that they should know
Help them stand
For what's right
The future belongs to them

Tinuke Aweda

_____

_____

_____

_____

_____

_____

_____

_____

_____

_____

_____

_____

_____

_____

_____

_____

_____

_____

_____

_____

_____

_____

_____

_____

_____

_____

_____

_____

_____

_____

_____

_____

_____

_____

_____

_____

_____

_____

_____

_____

_____

THE CREED

I laugh
I dance
I cheer
With a loud voice
Shouting it out from within, from the depth of my very
existence
It unites us, it defines us
It existed before we came, it will remain after we leave
The only difference is in its intensity
Tell its story to all who care to listen
So generations after us will know about it
They will understand that it is not about convenience, it is
about principle
It's not about innovation, it's about legacy
It's not about globalization, its about individualism
So while we can
While we have the power to influence
While we have the memories to tell our stories, let us do
so
Tell the world about the beginning
The traditions, the beliefs, the culture
Though unique, there is a cord that unites each one to
stand tall and proud
To hold fast to their individualism and their origin
To share the knowledge freely
To keep the creed alive

_____

_____

_____

_____

_____

_____

_____

_____

_____

_____

_____

_____

_____

_____

_____

_____

_____

_____

_____

_____

_____

WHERE IS THE SOUND

The sound of laughter
The sound of victory
The sound of children playing
The sound of celebrations
The sound of cheer and encouragement
Where did they all go
I stand and listen, waiting to hear those sounds
Often times the sound starts and then suddenly with cau-
tion stops mid way
Everyone is so mindful of their words, their actions and
their thoughts
There is no freedom of expression anymore
Gone are the days doors to houses were left unlocked
When people could celebrate success stories
When people could laugh and be merry
Those days are gone
When will they return?
When will they come back?
Are they gone with the wind or is it a function of time

_____

_____

_____

_____

_____

_____

_____

_____

_____

_____

_____

_____

_____

_____

_____

_____

_____

_____

_____

_____

_____

_____

_____

_____

_____

_____

_____

_____

_____

_____

_____

_____

_____

_____

_____

_____

_____

_____

_____

_____

_____

_____

_____

_____

_____

_____

_____

_____

_____

_____

Printed in the United States
By Bookmasters